Test Your
Business English
Marketing

Simon Sweeney

Series Editor: Nick Brieger

PENGUIN BOOKS

To Mum and Dad with love

PENGUIN BOOKS

Published by the Penguin Group
Penguin Books Ltd, 27 Wrights Lane, London W8 5TZ, England
Penguin Books USA Inc., 375 Hudson Street, New York, New York 10014, USA
Penguin Books Australia Ltd, Ringwood, Victoria, Australia
Penguin Books Canada Ltd, 10 Alcorn Avenue, Toronto, Ontario, Canada M4V 3B2
Penguin Books (NZ) Ltd, 182–190 Wairau Road, Auckland 10, New Zealand

Penguin Books Ltd, Registered Offices: Harmondsworth, Middlesex, England

Published by Penguin Books 1996
10 9 8 7 6 5 4 3 2 1

Text copyright © Simon Sweeney 1996
Illustrations copyright © Neville Swaine 1996
All rights reserved

The moral right of the author and of the illustrator has been asserted

Printed in England by Clays Ltd, St Ives plc
Set in 9.25/13.5pt Monophoto Times

Acknowledgements

I would like to thank the following people who have helped with research and with the work that went into preparing the manuscript: John Hinman, who helped with early research and provided important background information, Steve Flinders of York Associates, Steve Hick of Linguacraft, Clare Munden of Teamwork Marketing for help with some key terms, John Murphy of Interbrand plc and Barry Jones of the Boston Consulting Group.

I also want to thank Nick Brieger, the series editor, for advice, encouragement and numerous recommendations. Finally, I am most grateful to Hermione Ieronymidis, who copy-edited the manuscript and made many important suggestions that led to key improvements in the final version.

Needless to say, whatever weaknesses remain are mine and none of the above is remotely responsible for any of them.

INTRODUCTION

Language knowledge and communication skills are the basic tools for developing competence in a foreign language. Vocabulary, together with a command of grammar and pronunciation, are the main components of language knowledge.

This series aims to develop the vocabulary required by professionals and pre-service students. The materials provide clear and simple tests of around 500 key concepts and terms in various professional areas. Each book is devoted to one professional area, divided into eight sections. Each section, focusing on one topic area, tests the knowledge of both concepts and terms. The materials can be used as part of a language course for specialists or as a handy reference for self-study.

For the first books, we have chosen areas which are of significant current interest in the business world. Each has been written by an author with considerable practical experience in the field, and we hope that the series will prove a valuable aid to users.

ABOUT THIS BOOK

Test Your Business English: Marketing is for people working in marketing who are not native speakers of English. It aims to help them:
- check their knowledge of basic concepts and key terms (words and expressions) used in their professional area
- see how these terms are used so that they can use them effectively and successfully themselves.

The book will also be a useful source of information for trainers who need to run courses for marketing personnel.

The material has been designed for self-study or classroom use by learners at intermediate level or above.

Organization of the material

The book is divided into eight sections and each section deals with an important part of marketing management. In this way it is organized more like a textbook than a test book, with individual sections devoted to individual areas. We have chosen to do this so that, if they wish, learners can work through each section and see how terms group together. We believe this will help learners develop their range of expression in a structured and systematic way.

After the tests, there is:
- a complete answer key
- a full A-Z word list.

Using the material

The Contents page shows the eight main areas covered. Learners can either work through the book from the beginning or select sections according to their interests or needs. After each test, learners should check their answers. While working on a test, learners may come across unknown or unfamiliar words. This is an opportunity for them to check their understanding and extend their knowledge. So, a good dictionary of general English and a dictionary of marketing will be useful companions to this volume. In this way, the material in this book can be used both for testing and for teaching.

Selection of the terms

The terms are directly relevant to the work of people working in marketing. General terms are not included, nor are very technical terms. Only in Section 1 are more basic terms included where we think that their understanding is important to the understanding of other more specialized terms. The language model is predominantly British English.

CONTENTS

1 Key words 1

Find 9 common words connected with marketing in the word square. You can read the words vertically (3 words), horizontally (5 words) or diagonally (1 word). (See example):

R	Q	A	I	J	K	L	M	P	L	A	N
C	U	S	T	O	M	E	R	N	P	O	Q
S	A	A	M	A	R	K	E	T	I	N	G
H	L	B	L	F	G	H	J	T	S	T	O
O	I	F	E	F	W	R	U	U	C	V	O
J	T	G	A	G	Y	B	B	C	E	A	D
L	Y	H	T	H	I	R	U	B	D	U	S
N	Q	R	P	R	O	D	U	C	T	Q	P
O	S	I	T	T	R	V	G	H	J	W	R
O	M	S	E	R	V	I	C	E	S	X	E
D	I	K	I	R	E	S	E	A	R	C	H
D	X	X	A	P	Q	U	A	N	A	F	H

2 Definitions

Fill in the missing words in the sentences below. Choose from the following. One word is used twice.

customers	place	product	service
developing	price	profit	time
distribute	producing	promote	want
needs			

Marketing is concerned with getting the right (1) .... to the right (2) .... at the right (3) ....

Marketing is about meeting consumer (4) .... at a (5) ....

Marketing makes it easier for (6) .... to do business with you.

Booth D., *Principles of Strategic Marketing*
(Eastham, Merseyside: Tudor Publishing, 1990), pp. 31–7

Marketing aims to find out what people (7) ....; then (8) .... and (9) .... a (10) .... or (11) .... that will satisfy those wants; and then determining the best way to (12) ...., (13) .... and (14) .... the product or service.

Stanton W.J., *Fundamentals of Marketing* (McGraw Hill, 1981)
quoted in Evans D., *Marketing* (Oxford: Oxford University Press, 1990), p. 17

3 Word building

Fill in the missing words in the table.

	Verb	Personal noun	General noun
1		marketer	
2	distribute		
3			competition
4			advertising, advertisement
5		supplier	
6		sponsor	
7	consume		
8	produce		
9		analyst	
10		researcher	
11	import		

4 A new market

M & T Cables wants to enter a new market. Read the following letter to a possible export partner. Fill in the missing words in the sentences. Choose from the following:

analysis	free	mix	research
demand	goods	plan	trends

M & T Cables GmbH
Lindacher Str.48 · D-40474 Dusseldorf · Germany

Peter Jarrow
P.O. Box 320
Suva
FIJI
22 May 19—

Dear Peter,

Re. South Pacific Market

Thank you for your letter about your plans to market our products in the South Pacific region. As you know, we want to sell our (1) .... in every (2) .... market in the world, so naturally we are interested in your region.
Obviously we have to do some market (3) ....
For now, I have four questions:

1. How is the present supply and (4) .... for our kind of products?

2. What kind of marketing (5) .... do you think we should develop in our marketing (6) ....?

3. What are the market (7) .... in this sector?

4. Can you recommend someone to carry out a detailed market (8) .... for us?

I look forward to hearing from you as soon as possible.

Yours sincerely,

Sandra Sah

Sandra Sah

5 Choose the word

Choose the word or phrase with the same meaning as the definition.

1 Providing money to cultural or sporting activities in exchange for advertising rights.
   a promotion   b grant aid   c sponsorship

2 A business which specializes in giving advice and support to companies about marketing and markets.
   a marketing consultancy b counselling service   c company analysts

3 An economy which allows open and reasonably free exchange between private companies.
   a command economy   b conservative economy   c free market economy

4 A market in which there are too many suppliers producing similar products.
   a saturated market   b buyers' market   c heavy market

5 A market in which there are few suppliers producing goods that a lot of people want to buy.
   a weak market   b sellers' market   c light market

6 A company which sells more of a particular type of product than its competitors.
   a trend setter   b multinational   c market leader

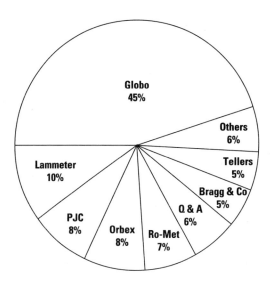

7 A person with specialist knowledge of a specific market who often predicts what will happen and tries to explain what has happened.

   a market analyst   b forecaster   c market broker

8 A specific promotional activity over a limited period of time.

   a campaign   b season   c trend

9 The activity of moving goods from the producer to the consumer.

   a shipment   b distribution   c orientation

10 The activity of selling goods to other countries.

   a multinational   b exporting   c exchange
      distribution

11 The proportion of the total market which one company controls.

   a dominion   b market place   c market share

6 Planning

Look at the internal memo below and fill in the missing words. Choose from the following:

mix	plan	strengths
opportunities	price	threats
packaging	product	weaknesses
place	promotion	

SANDERMAN & KELLS Ltd

```
MEMO

From: AB
To:   DG

Re. Marketing policy

Success depends on good marketing. We need a clear strategy to
develop understanding of:
1. our present position
2. marketing strategy

We must build a new marketing (1) ............... . This should
be based on a clear SWOT analysis, i.e. understanding of the
present market position in terms of:
* (2) ................
* (3) ................
* (4) ................
* (5) ................

We must develop a seven point marketing (6) ................,
describing:
* (7) ................
* (8) ................
* (9) ................
* (10) ................
* (11) ................
* People
* Phasing

I suggest you send a report to John as soon as possible.

Call me to discuss.
```

Andrew

```
Andrew
```

7 The seven *Ps*

Fill in the missing words in this description of the marketing mix.

The traditional marketing mix was described in terms of four *Ps*:

1 P ...., the goods or services

2 P ...., the cost of the product

3 P ...., often called distribution

4 P ...., which aims to make people aware of the product.

In recent years other considerations have been added, giving a mix of at least seven *Ps*:

5 P ...., or everyone involved from producer to consumer

6 P ...., which means the wrapper or the box the product comes in, but also all added-value and intangible assets

7 P ...., or everything to do with time.

8 The marketing mix

Peter Glass of Citimetal Ltd is talking to Anna Price, a marketing consultant. Complete Anna's part of the conversation. Choose from the following:

---

a And then the fourth area is phasing.

b It covers both goods and services offered by the company.

c Exactly – and the desire to buy the product. And, finally, people, which means colleagues, employees, agents and customers. The idea is to keep everyone happy, make personal contact.

d Yes, or timing – getting things where they should be at the right time.

e The second area is place – also called distribution – meaning the movement of goods from the producer to the consumer.

f Well, we identified five areas where improvement is necessary.

g After place, packaging. Packaging includes the packaging materials but, more importantly, all types of added value and customer expectations.

h The first is product.

i Promotion.

Peter: So, what have you got to report?

Anna: ....
....

Peter: Really? What are they?

Anna: ....
....

Peter: And what exactly does that term cover?

Anna: ....
....

Peter: I see. What else?

Anna: ....
....

Peter: And after place, what's next?

Anna: ....

         ....

Peter: Yes, I understand – the extra things that customers want.

Anna: ....

         ....

Peter: Phasing?

Anna: ....

         ....

Peter: Delivery on time. Right, I follow you. And what's the next area?

Anna: ....

         ....

Peter: So, that's creating consumer awareness and establishing the brand
         identity?

Anna: ....

         ....

9 Key words 2

Write the number of each description (1–10) and the letter of the correct picture (a–j) next to each word or phrase in the box. (See example):

augmented product	5.9
clone	.....
consumer durable	.....
core product	.....
fast moving consumer goods	.....
generic product	.....
perishables	.....
primary manufacturing	.....
sell-by date	.....
service	.....

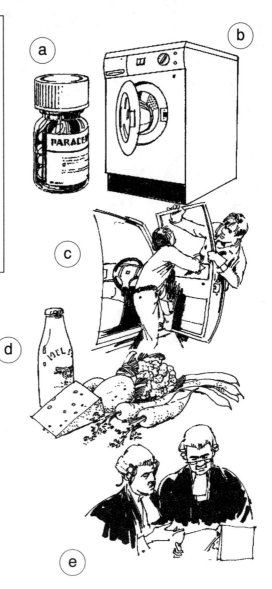

1 Organic products, usually food, that will go bad after a certain amount of time.

2 Products sold in very large quantities, such as groceries. They are bought often and move through stores quickly.

3 A new product, especially in the computer industry, which is almost the same as a successful one made by a more famous manufacturer.

4 Long-lasting products produced and sold in large quantities.

5 A basic product with additional features and services added to the total package.

6 A basic product which is bought because of a particular need, e.g. a drink for thirst.

7 Products which are not known by a brand name, e.g. pharmaceutical products like paracetamol for headaches.

8 Specialist expertise or advice to help companies or individuals in, e.g. legal matters, marketing.

9 A time suggested for reasons of safety by which perishable goods should be used.

10 The actual making of products or components for products.

10 Branding

A Rearrange the letters to find words that are connected with branding.

1 nbard yitnedit   ....

2 ardnb eman   ....

3 dabrn igema   ....

4 won-drabn   ....

5 radbn nataviluo   ....

6 burnadden   ....

7 antilbinge stases   ....

8 yallyot   ....

9 rempuim barnd   ....

B Fill in the missing words in the sentences. Use words from part A.

1 Coca Cola, Sony and Mercedes Benz are all famous brand ....s.

2 Deciding a financial value for a brand name is called brand ....

3 Consumers usually expect to pay less for products that are ....

4 Products like Chanel or Christian Dior have a brand .... which is more glamorous than that of many less well-known competitors.

5 In the 1990s most supermarkets began to sell .... products.

6 A brand name is valuable not only for the main products that are represented by the name, but also for a complete range of .... assets that accompany that name.

7 A key concern for marketers is to establish brand .... among their customers so that they do not buy similar products made by other companies.

8 Consumers are often prepared to pay high prices for .... brands which they believe represent high quality.

9 A new product must create a brand .... so that it is easily recognized and associated with specific qualities.

11 Product marketing

Choose the best definition for each of the words or phrases.

1 *an augmented product*
   a a product now selling at a higher price
   b a product that is no longer made
   c the core product plus additional benefits such as brand name, quality styling and design features, extended warranty, after-sales service, etc.

2 *generic*
   a not known by a special brand name
   b for general use
   c popular with all types of consumers

3 *cannibalism*
   a where a product eats into competitors' market share
   b where a product reduces sales of other products made by the same manufacturer
   c where an employee leaves his/her company to join a competitor

4 *the sell-by date*
   a the limit placed on sales representatives to meet targets
   b the date by which a food or drug must be sold
   c the date on which a product is sold

5 *launch*
   a when a product is taken off the market
   b when a product is tested before being sold
   c when a product is first released onto the market

6 *the product life cycle*
   a the normal pattern of sales for a product
   b the process of development of a new product
   c the different stages of improvement in an old product

7 *part*
   a a product
   b a component
   c a phase in the development of a product

12 Selling

Jan Groot, marketing manager for TPC Inc., is making a presentation to the company's sales staff. Write the number of each picture in the box in the correct part of the speech.

Our R & D department designed the Triple X PC48655 over a five-year period ... ☐

... and the product was finally launched this year. ☐

The core product is, of course, a personal computer ... ☐

... but the augmented package includes four types of software, five product manuals, a self-help guide, free on-site warranty and the prestige of the Triple X brand name. ☐

Of course, all components used in the manufacture of the Triple X PC48655 have been well tested. ☐

We offer a full after-sales service ... ☐

... and extended five-year warranty with absolute confidence. ☐

Furthermore, we expect the product to experience rapid early sales for at least three years ... ☐

... before being joined by me-too products from our competitors. ☐

13 After-sales assistance

The following is from a flyer which came with a new telephone. Fill in the missing words and phrases in the sentences. Choose from the following:

after-sales	labour	parts
customer	launched	state-of-the-art
helpline	network	warranty

Since the **TT150** was (1) ...., it has been an outstanding success. Well known for reliability, it does, however, come with a full two-year (2) .... and (3) .... (4) .... Utilizing the very latest technology, this (5) .... product is supported by our extensive (6) .... (7) .... Call our (8) .... (9) .... for free advice on how to solve any problems you may have.

14 Products, services and service

Fill in the missing words in the sentences by changing the word in **bold** type on the right. (See example):

1 We sell a very large range of goods, including fast moving
   <u>Consumer</u> goods such as canned foods, cleaning
   materials and cassettes.   **consume**

2 Of course, we also sell .... goods like milk, cheese
   and meat, with a sell-by date of only a few days.   **perish**

3 It is not only food .... which have a very short
   shelf life.   **produce**

4 For larger consumer ...., like hi-fi and TVs, we
   also have to provide an after-sales service.   **duration**

5 An important aspect of marketing goods like CD players
   and televisions is possible .... value, such as free
   videos or CDs.   **add**

6 The business of a .... is to sell products.   **retail**

7 A .... industry is one that offers specialist
   expertise or advice. Lawyers, marketers, translators and
   financiers all do this.   **serve**

8 If you are not completely satisfied with any product
   .... in this store, you may return it and receive a
   complete refund or exchange it for a different product.   **purchaser**

9 A .... is a licence to produce a product.
   The inventor may sell or lease it to a manufacturer.   **patented**

10 A product which was expensive to develop, manufacture
   and launch, and which does not have the sales that the
   manufacturer expected can be described as a .... **flopped**

15 Product management

Write the number of each picture next to the correct product management term.

product failure	.....
product life cycle	.....
launch	.....
positioning	.....
product mix	.....
product classification	.....

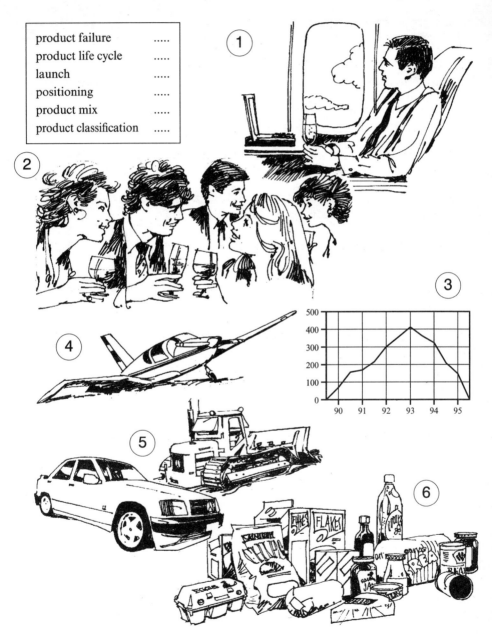

16 Success and failure

Fill in the missing words in the sentences. Choose from the following:

away	by	off	onto
back	into	on	to

1 Perishable goods go .... in a short time.

2 If dairy products are not sold .... the sell-by date, they cannot be offered for sale.

3 Unsold perishable goods usually have to be thrown ....

4 If a safety fault is discovered in an electrical product, the manufacturer has to take .... all faulty examples of the product.

5 Thousand of new products are put .... the market every day, but only a few are successful.

6 Success or failure depends .... many factors, but the most important is the quality of the marketing.

7 Customers with a strong sense of brand loyalty are rarely prepared to switch .... a new competitor.

8 Powerful advertising may help a new product to eat .... the market share of rival brands.

17 Key words 3

Find 8 common words connected with price in the word square. You can read the words vertically (4 words) or horizontally (4 words), forwards or backwards.

A	P	R	I	C	E	L	T
D	I	S	C	O	U	N	T
E	C	R	G	S	N	O	I
M	P	O	R	T	E	V	F
A	W	R	M	S	V	I	O
N	I	P	F	E	E	O	R
D	R	L	M	H	R	G	P
A	M	A	R	G	I	N	E

18 Fixing a price

A Match each word on the left with a word on the right.

1 penetration		a)	demand
2 down-		b)	priced
3 fixed		c)	market
4 budget		d)	costs
5 elastic		e)	strategy

B Now make another five phrases opposite in meaning to those in part A.

1 inelastic		a)	demand
2 variable		b)	priced
3 premium		c)	market
4 skimming		d)	costs
5 up-		e)	strategy

19 Pricing policy

Read the summary of a report on a meeting about pricing policy in Callan Ltd, a manufacturing company. Think what the words in **bold** type mean. Then mark sentences 1–11 True or False. If a sentence is false, explain why.

Report

Subject: Marketing Focus Group Meeting

Date: 4 December 19..

Present: DF, HT, PT, JF

The following decisions were taken regarding pricing strategy for the new year.

i. **Budget priced goods** shall only be sold in Category 'C' stores. Goods can only be sold at a budget price where they have already been offered at the **recommended retail price** for a period of not less than three months.

ii. Agents shall be instructed that from January 1, we do not allow **discounts** on any goods not sold at a previously higher price for a period of three months.

iii. Decisions on pricing must realize **margins** for the retailer of up to 25%. Prices below 15% are unlikely to be **economic** for any of our retailers.

iv. Similarly, our own **factory gate price** must allow the company to cover all **production costs** and also to realize a profit of between 25 and 35%. Our marketing team should watch the **market prices** to ensure that we do not price ourselves above the **going rate**.

v. Wherever possible, we should sell our products to retailers. This will cut out intermediaries and avoid **retail prices** being forced higher by high **wholesale prices**.

	True	False
1 **Budget priced goods** are sold at a lower price than they were offered at before.	☐	☑
2 The **recommended retail price** is the price the manufacturer thinks a retailer should charge for a product.	☐	☐
3 A **discount** is a reduced price offered after a period on offer at a higher price.	☐	☐
4 The **margin** is the difference between the cost of a product to a manufacturer or retailer and the price the manufacturer or retailer receives when the product is sold.	☐	☐
5 An **economic price** is a price that allows a reasonable profit.	☐	☐
6 The **factory gate price** is the cost of producing the product for the factory.	☐	☐
7 **Production costs** are the expenses a manufacturer has to pay for labour.	☐	☐
8 The **market price** is the price one company charges for a product.	☐	☐
9 The **going rate** is the price the consumers are prepared to pay.	☐	☐
10 **Retail price** is the price consumers actually pay.	☐	☐
11 The **wholesale price** is the price paid by consumers who buy many examples of the same product.	☐	☐

20 Pricing strategy 1

Fill in the missing phrases in the sentences. Choose from the following:

budget priced	going rate	retail margin	unit cost
demand curve	price war	selling costs	

1 The amount of money necessary to produce one individual example of a product is the ....

2 The difference in price between what retailers pay for a product and what they sell the product at is called the ....

3 The total amount of money spent on all aspects of selling, including advertising, commissions and promotion, is known as the ....

4 A period during which several competitors aggressively lower their prices in an effort to build up market share is called a ....

5 Products at the lowest end of the price scale are sometimes referred to as .... goods.

6 The price for a product or for services which the market will accept is the ....

7 The line on a graph which shows the relationship between prices and consumer demand is called the ....

21 Pricing strategy 2

Match the words (1–7) with the definitions (a–g).

1 break-even point

   a) The price wholesalers and distributors pay for goods.

2 discounting

   b) A pricing strategy based on low pricing and low unit profits.

3 factory gate price

   c) The point in the development of a product when sales begin to exceed the investment.

4 inelastic demand

   d) Consumers who are very attentive to price changes and look for lower-priced items.

5 overheads

   e) Sales of a product do not change much with variations in price.

6 penetration strategy

   f) Reducing prices from a level at which the product was previously offered for sale.

7 price sensitive buyers

   g) The day-to-day costs of running a business.

22 Costs

Choose the best definition for each of the words or phrases.

1 *cost of labour*
a cost of all work involved in making a product or service ready for sale
b cost of manual workers employed by a company
c cost of industrial action by employees

2 *cost of production*
a selling price for a finished product
b all expenses for raw materials, heating, lighting, electricity, etc.
c all costs involved in making a product ready for distribution and sale

3 *cost of sales*
a total costs involved in making a product or service, distributing it and selling it
b cost of selling a product in salaries, commissions, etc.
c the price of a product when it is sold

4 *commission*
a a royalty paid to an inventor of a product
b a percentage of the selling price which is paid to the seller, usually an agent or distributor
c instructions given to a sales representative or to the shop which is asked to sell a product

5 *selling costs*
a the total money raised selling a product or service
b the costs involved in distributing, promoting and selling a product
c the salaries and other expenses paid to the sales representatives

6 *direct costs*
a all costs relating to production of a product, including development costs and raw materials, electricity and labour
b all taxes paid to the government
c the cost of labour involved in making a product

7 *direct labour costs*

a all costs relating to production of a product, including development costs and raw materials, electricity and labour

b all labour costs involved in actual production of a product

c all labour costs involved in producing a product and, in addition, all support labour costs, such as secretarial and administrative work

8 *fixed costs*

a prices established by the government

b costs which are decided by the management of a manufacturing company, not by suppliers or retailers

c costs which do not depend on quantity of production, e.g. heating, lighting, rent

9 *variable costs*

a costs which change according to the quantity of production, such as raw materials, components, overtime pay, etc.

b costs which are difficult to estimate as they may suddenly change because of changes in the market, such as competitors' pricing

c costs which change according to the time of the year, e.g. warm clothes for winter or summer fashions

10 *overheads*

a regular costs associated with the day-to-day running of a company

b additional expenses because of a higher than expected demand for products

c extra costs above what was planned in the costs budget

11 *unit cost*

a the costs associated with all production of all products

b the costs involved in making one single example of a product

c the total costs for any one part of a factory producing one type of product

12 *labour input*

a the cost of labour in producing products for distribution and sale

b additional payments to workers during periods of high demand

c the costs of all non-managerial wages and salaries

23 Aggressive pricing

Read the newspaper report about SAWA, a computer game company which is introducing a new low-priced product to help win a bigger market share. Then fill in the missing phrases in the sentences. Choose from the following:

advanced orders	high penetration	production costs
break even	premium price	recommended retail
factory gate	price war	

SAWA in low price game

The Japanese computer games company SAWA is planning an October launch for a new game called Zappo. The development of the game has taken two years but (1) .... are impressive. The company expects the product to (2) .... within one year. (3) .... are low as the labour input in this sector is relatively small.

Margins in computer games are usually high, but SAWA has promised a (4) .... strategy, with a competitive pricing policy.

This is a change of policy for SAWA, whose products have always carried a (5) ...., SAWA being a relatively exclusive brand.

The (6) .... price is expected to be around $45, with the (7) .... price being around 33% of that. Such a low price may have the effect of creating a (8) .... in the computer games market.

A further point of interest is that SAWA predict a long shelf-life for Zappo, perhaps five years, which is longer than normal in this sector.

24 Who's who?

Fill in the crossword. The answers are all people involved in the movement of goods from the producer to the consumer.

1 This person sells products on behalf of one or more producers.

2 Responsibility for moving goods from producer to retailer is this person's job.

3 This person travels around persuading retailers to stock products.

4 When you want to buy a product, you go to this person.

5 Another word for this person's job is middleman.

6 Small shops often have to buy from this person.

7 This is the person who sells specialist products.

8 Someone who sells goods to other countries is called this.

9 The person who buys a product.

10 The person who uses a product, including food and drink.

11 The person who uses a product other than food and drink.

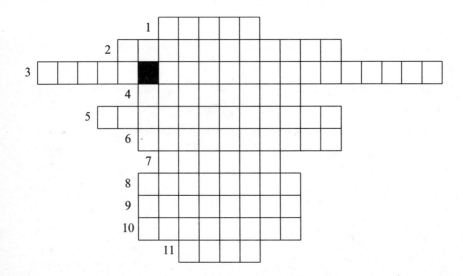

25 People and places

Write the number of each picture next to the correct word or words.

air freight operator	.....
door-to-door salesperson	.....
haulage contractor	.....
hypermarket	.....
production plant	.....
retailer	.....
shipping line	.....
telesales operator	.....
wholesaler	.....

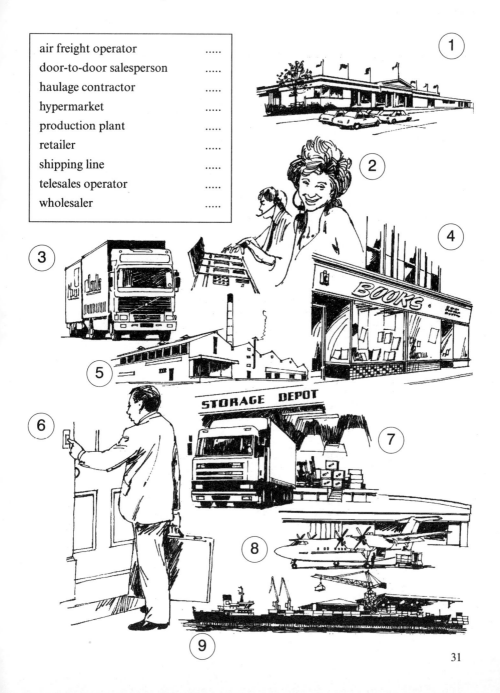

26 The distribution chain

Replace the underlined words in the fax below with a word with the same or a similar meaning. Write the number next to the word. Choose from the following. (See example):

consumers	**2**	multiples	sales forces .....
despatch		producer	sales representatives .....
middlemen		retailers	wholesalers .....

F A X

Call if message is not clear

TELEPHONE: 00-33-1-43438492
FAX NUMBER: 33 1 43437319
To: Sara Alessi
From: Alain Bouzier
Subject: Distribution system

As the (1) <u>manufacturer</u>, we obviously must ensure that products reach (2) <u>customers</u> with maximum efficiency. Now, we use independent (3) <u>distributors</u>, but we should consider better alternatives. The following changes need urgent consideration:

* Cutting out (4) <u>intermediaries</u> — this would bring cost savings.
* Larger (5) <u>sales teams</u>.
* Many more (6) <u>reps</u>.
* Improved (7) <u>shipment</u> systems.
* Closer relationships with (8) <u>dealers</u>.
* More links with (9) <u>chains</u>.

Call to discuss.
Regards,

Alain

Alain

---

27 Classical distribution channel

Fill in the missing labels on the flow chart. Choose from the following:

agent	haulage company	sales representative
customer	producer	
distributor	retailer	

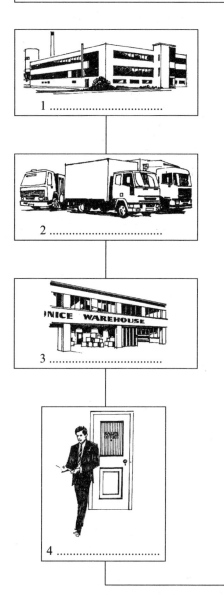

1 ....

2 ....

3 ....

4 ....

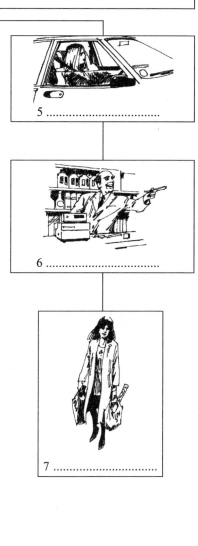

5 ....

6 ....

7 ....

28 Shipping methods

Write the number of each picture next to the correct method of transportation.

air freight	.....
barge	.....
container ship	.....
despatch rider	.....
rail freight	.....
road haulage	.....

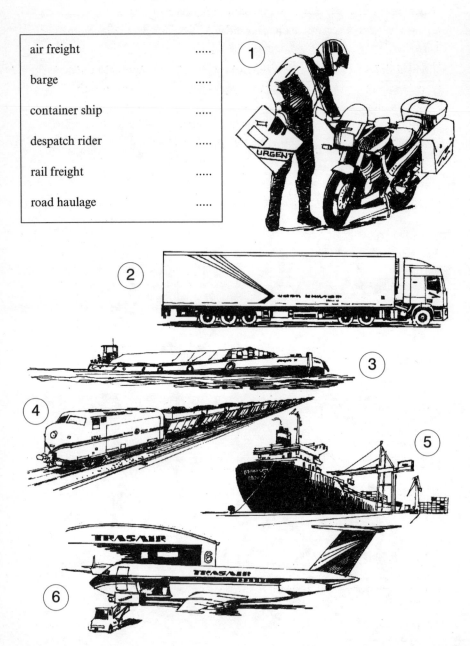

29 Retail outlets and systems

Replace the words in italic type in each of the newspaper extracts. Write the answers under the extracts. Choose from the following. (See example):

chain stores	hypermarkets	specialist retailers
cold calling	large multiples	telesales staff
commission	mail order	warehouses
door-to-door selling	mail order companies	
franchises	purchasing power	

(1) *Companies which specialize in selling goods through a catalogue sent out through the post* normally have (2) *large buildings full of goods* from where the goods are despatched.

1 ~~mail order companies~~

2 ....

(3) *Companies which own many stores* have (4) *strength in negotiating prices* where manufacturers are concerned. Small shops do not have this.

3 ....

4 ....

(5) *Retail outlets which pay a licence fee to trade under a famous brand name* often benefit from increased business, since the name is a powerful advertisement.

5 ....

(6) *Going from one house to another, knocking on doors* is a highly labour-intensive type of sales operation. This type of work is normally paid on the basis of a (7) *percentage of the sales achieved being paid to the seller.* Another type of selling is by (8) *a combination of catalogue and ordering by post*. This may be complemented by (9) *personnel who sell by telephone*, trained to deal with customers' calls. Another kind of telephone selling is through (10) *telephoning someone who is not expecting your call but whom you think might buy your product*. The idea is to get your prospective customer to agree to buy your products or receive a home visit for a demonstration.

6 ....

7 ....

8 ....

9 ....

10 ....

(11) *Large out-of-town stores selling a huge range of goods* have had a serious effect on business for smaller, city centre shops. (12) *Small shops offering a personalized and highly specialized service* can survive better than small shops which try to compete directly with the larger outlets and other (13) *retail outlets owned by the same company and trading under the same name.*

11 ....

12 ....

13 ....

30 Distribution 1

Fill in the missing words in the sentences below. Choose from the following:

commission agent	franchise agreement	shipping line
container port	independent distributor	vending machine
distribution agreement	sales force	
electronic trading	shelf space	

1 An agent who receives a percentage of the sales is a ....

2 An agreement to sell only one manufacturer's goods is called a sole ....

3 All the people involved in selling a company's goods or services are the ....

4 A place where ships are loaded with special metal boxes full of goods is called a ....

5 .... s buy from companies and sell to retailers.

6 Trading through computers, with orders and payment transmitted along telephone network, is called ....

7 The amount of space given over in a shop for displaying a particular product is called ....

8 An agreement to pay a licence fee to use a well-known name is called a ....

9 A machine in which you put coins to buy confectionery or other small items is called a ....

10 A company that owns a lot of ships is called a ....

31 Distribution 2

Here is an extract from a marketing consultant's report on distribution systems in the fast moving consumer goods (FMCG) sector. The report describes three distribution systems. Write the number of each description next to the correct system.

vertical marketing system (VMS)　　☐

conventional marketing system (CMS)　　☐

total systems approach (TSA)　　☐

Distribution systems

We can identify three main distribution systems:

1　Traditionally there used to be a line consisting of independent producers, wholesalers and retailers. Each was a separate business.

2　Now, many businesses work together in a unified system where producers, wholesalers and retailers act together. They may be under common ownership, or they have contracted to work together as a single system.

3　However, a new trend is a distribution system which is designed to accommodate consumer needs at minimum cost, and places every step of the distribution channel under a single control.

Conclusion

In reality, the benefits to consumers of a simplified distribution process may not be as great as one might have thought. However, company profits can certainly rise.

32 Key Words 4

Write the number of the picture next to the correct word or phrase.

commercial	.....	point-of-sale advertising	.....
competition	.....	reply coupon	.....
discount	.....	slogan	.....
mailing list	.....	target audience	.....
mass media	.....		

(1) *Crystal Communication makes communication crystal clear.*

(2) If I buy 200, will you give me a better price?

(3)

SD Financial Services

Yes please! Send me further details of the complete Home Finance Plan.

Name: ....

Address: ....

....

....

Telephone: (home) .... (work) ....

④

⑤

⑥

⑦

⑧

⑨

WASH ALL WASHES BEST....

Araldi, V. Via Dante 38, San Giorgio a Cremano (NA)

Arcometti, P. Corso Occidentale 42, Pisa (PI)

Arione, G. Via Garabaldi 2, La Morra (CN)

Armando Dino, Via Stretta 10, San Gimingnano (FI)

Assenzi P. Piazza della Libertà 32, Treviso (TV)

Attametti, F. Via della Cantina 22, Trastevere, Roma

33 Planning advertising

SPEAR, a mail order company, is planning a new advertising campaign. Below is an extract from an internal report to senior marketers in the company. Fill in the missing words and phrases in the report. Choose from the following:

advertisements	commercials	hard sell
advertising mix	competition	impulse buying
campaign	consumer awareness	mail shot
catalogue	direct mail	

ADVERTISING PLAN

Our plan is to sell products through a (1) .... and mail order service. We will use a high pressure, (2) .... approach. We can attract customers to order the goods by offering special (3) .... prizes. Once the catalogue arrives, consumers will order goods which have an instant appeal: we will depend on (4) ....

Another approach is to run a long advertising (5) .... to increase (6) .... of our products. We plan a variety of advertising techniques: this (7) .... will consist of television (8) ...., newspaper (9) ...., and street advertising. We have a good target customer database, so we will use (10) .... We plan to do a (11) .... twice, to put extra pressure on those who do not answer the first time.

34 Strategies 1

Match each strategy 1–7 with the correct description a–g.

1 A promotion strategy based on getting
the consumer's attention and interest,
then desire for the product, then action
(buying the product).

a) generic advertising

2 All forms of advertising except mass
media advertising.

b) below-the-line
   promotion

3 Mass media advertising.

c) AIDA

4 A selling style based on identifying
and meeting the customer's needs.

d) customer-oriented
   selling

5 Advertising for a whole sector, such
as tourism or health promotion,
rather than for a specific product.

e) push strategy

6 A sales-oriented selling style, using
high pressure and persuasion,
discounts and free services.

f) above-the-line
   promotion

7 A method of sales promotion which
uses pressure on distributors or on retailers.

g) hard sell approach

35 Strategies 2

Fill in the missing words in the sentences. Choose from the following:

consumers	publicity	unique selling
emotional appeal	rational appeal	proposition
promotes	targets	

Yes!

Only
New Denta
has the right formula to
protect milk teeth
AND
keep them
absolutely clean!

1 A set of characteristics that make a product different to its competitors is its
....

2 Any activity which increases consumer awareness of a company or its products
is ....

TECHNICAL SPECIFICATIONS

Focal length:	50mm	Max aperture lock:	Provided
Maximum aperture:	f/1.8	Diaphragm:	Fully automatic
Lens construction:	6 elements in 5 groups	Exposure measurement:	Via full aperture method
Picture angle:	46°		with A1 cameras: via stop
Distance scale:	Graduated in metres and feet		down method with non-A1
	from 0.45m (1.75ft) to infinity		cameras
Aperture scale:	f/1.8 to f/22 on both standard	Mount:	Bayonet mount
	and aperture direct readout	Attachment size:	52mm (P=0.75mm)
	scales	Weight:	Approx 155g

3 Promotional techniques based on giving the consumer facts and technical information are concerned with ....

4 Promotional techniques aimed at people's fears, ambition, feelings, likes and dislikes are concerned with ....

5 Advertising .... consumers and .... products.

6 Mass media promotion aims to influence public perception, not only target ....

36 Types of promotion

Choose the correct alternative for each sentence.

1 **direct mailing / mail order**

Sending product or service information by post to specific individuals or companies is called ....

2 **personal selling / direct selling**

A selling technique based on making a personal call to an individual or company is called ....

3 **in-store promotion / special offer**

A promotion based on advertising in the actual shop is an ....

4 **point-of-sale advertising / on-pack promotion**

A promotion method that involves the packaging of a product, such as including a free sample or coupons is called ....

5 **sponsorship / perimeter advertising**

Advertising around the playing area at sports grounds is called ....

6 **bargain selling / BOGOF**

A promotion method for fast-moving-consumer-goods which involves buying one and getting one free is called ....

37 Product promotion

Write the number of each picture next to the correct type of promotion.

banner towing	.....
billboard	.....
freebie	.....
offer	.....
sandwich board	.....
sponsorship	.....
T-shirt advertising	.....
TV commercial	.....

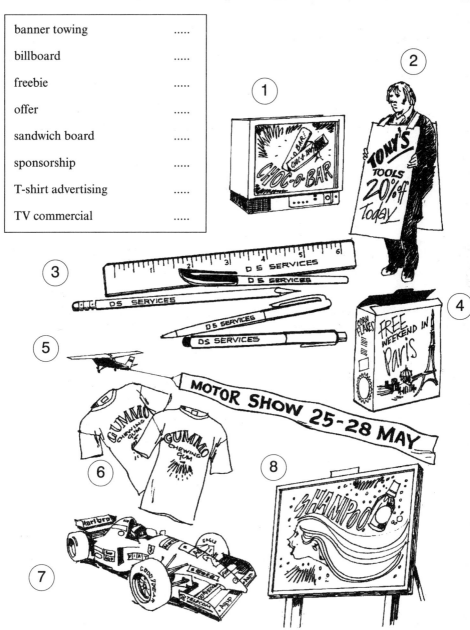

38 Promoting a message

Match the definitions (1–6) with the phrases (a–f).

1 The way the company is perceived by the public.

    a) positioning

2 What a promotion says about its subject.

    b) message structure

3 The attempt by marketers to give a product a unique strength, or special characteristics, in the market.

    c) message format

4 The one who conveys the message in the advertisement.

    d) corporate image

5 The way a message is presented in an advertisement, for example through symbols, through shock, through humour.

    e) message source

6 The design of an advertisement, in terms of presenting a problem, providing a solution and justifying why that solution works.

    f) message content

39 Key words 5

Use the definitions to help you rearrange the letters to find words connected with market research.

1 A study of what people think or what they do.

   yesvur ....

2 A person who finds out information from the public in order to discover what they want or can afford to buy.

   kemrat charseerer ....

3 A set of questions to find out people's opinions on particular issues, often used in studies of political opinion and preference.

   lolp ....

4 Something that is given away free to make the customer aware of the product.

   plesma ....

5 A set of questions designed to find out what people think about a product or service.

   teronequinsia ....

6 Information collected from research. The researcher then analyses the information before making conclusions.

   atad ....

7 Subjectivity or personal preferences in how one collects information or analyses the results of a survey.

   saib ....

8 The person who is asked questions or is studied in market research.

   justceb ....

9 Another name for the person who answers questions in market research, often by returning a completed questionnaire.

   pestendron ....

40 Survey results

Look at the statistics collected from a survey. Then read the newspaper report of the results and mark statements 1–8 T (True) or F (False).

Method: Telephone

Age:		15	16	17	18	19	20
Social group:	A	3	9	12	14	12	12
	B	23	41	26	34	25	22
	C1	49	20	29	35	32	38
	C2	14	10	19	10	18	16
	D	6	12	6	2	10	4
	E	5	8	8	5	3	8

1 Is eating healthy food important for you?

	15	16	17	18	19	20
Yes	7	19	5	8	27	6
No	4	5	3	2	12	2

2 How often do you eat healthy food?

	15	16	17	18	19	20
Always	1	2	-	-	3	-
Most of the time	2	3	6	1	2	1
Sometimes	4	2	1	-	11	1
Rarely	1	3	1	7	14	2
Never	3	14	-	2	9	4

Survey shows young prefer healthy food

An omnibus survey carried out by Audience Research Limited for the Food Manufacturing Alliance, a food manufacturers' marketing group, has revealed that young people are increasingly concerned about healthy eating.

The survey, (1) ☐ *based on telephone interviews* using a (2) ☐ *random sample* of 1,200 teenagers (3) ☐ *aged 14–19,* showed that (4) ☐ *the majority, seventy-two per cent, thought eating healthy food was 'important' for them.* A much smaller percentage, (5) ☐ *twenty-five per cent, actually claimed that 'most of the time' they ate 'reasonably healthy food'.*

The report also showed marked variation in the results, depending on social status. Respondents' social status was assessed on the basis of parents' occupation. (6) ☐ *Higher status groups were clearly more interested in healthy eating.*

However, it was (7) ☐ *not possible to draw firm conclusions regarding the relationship between age and healthy eating,* as there is no consistent trend in the results.

The ARL research was criticized by Helen Shawcross of the Consumer Associaton, who said that the survey failed to offer proper guidance to young respondents on what actually constitutes healthy eating. She said the report was biased, since (8) ☐ *most of the respondents were in higher socio-economic groups.* She said the report could easily be used to defend the present marketing of unhealthy foods. 'A lot of food marketing specifically targets young people,' she said.

41 Market research objectives

A clothing manufacturer, Corallo, wants to know why its sales of jeans are falling at a rate of 10% a year. They have asked Abacus Data Research (ADR), a market research consultancy, to find out.

Replace each phrase in *italic* type in ADR's letter with a phrase of similar meaning. Write your answers on the lines below. Choose from the following:

advertising research	in-house research	population
causal research study	market research	questionnaire
consumer awareness	market research brief	representative
consumer panels	observational research	secondary research
consumer research	pilot questionnaire	

1	8 ....
2	9 ....
3	10 ....
4	11 ....
5	12 ....
6	13 ....
7	14 ....

ADR
Abacus Data Research

South Dakota Blvd., Englewood Cliffs, 07632 New Jersey

Sam Klein
Corallo Clothing Company
P.O. Box 230
Englewood Cliffs   May 20, 19..

Dear Sam,

Thank you for your letter dated May 15. As I said when we met briefly last week, we at ADR would be very pleased to help you with (1) *studies on your products and their markets*. What I need now is a detailed (2) *description of your objectives for this study* — a statement of exactly what you need to know.

If we set up a (3) *study that aims to explain a particular phenomenon*, in this case on why you are experiencing a sales fall, we should of course go direct to consumers and ask their opinions. This type of (4) *study of what consumers think* will be vital. We can do this in three ways:

1 Using (5) *groups of typical consumers that we bring together for detailed questioning*. The members of the panel need to be (6) *typical* of the whole (7) *mass* of jeans buyers.

2 A conventional (8) *paper with a lot of questions* sent out to consumers. Alone, this is less effective, even if we use a (9) *test set of questions* to make sure we are asking the right questions. But it is much cheaper.

3 We can use (10) *studies of actual sales*. But this kind of study is based on figures, rather than on what people say, so it gives only limited information.

A further area to think about is (11) *how much consumers actually know about your company and its products*. We can carry out some (12) *studies into the effects of your advertising*.

Please send us any (13) *studies you have carried out yourselves*, or any (14) *studies using published material* that you have used in the past. This will help our background investigations.

Looking forward to hearing from you.
Yours truly,

Robert R. McCawley
Deputy Vice-President

42 Types of research

Below are 11 types of market research, each followed by four statements. Two are true, two are false. Mark the statements T (True) or F (False). (See example):

1 *agency research*
a ..F.. It compares one agency with another.
b ..... It is carried out by independent agencies, usually experts in particular fields.
c ..... It is the opposite of in-house research.
d ..... It is research work for governments.

2 *clinical trial*
a ..... It is research carried out by clinical agencies.
b ..... It is research into the effects of drugs or treatment methods.
c ..... Pharmaceutical companies carry out clinical trials.
d ..... It is a test to find out if a finished product works.

3 *desk research*
a ..... It is research carried out using published material.
b ..... It can include information about geography, politics, economics and social conditions.
c ..... It involves going out to ask consumers for their opinions.
d ..... It is the study of research results using computer analysis.

4 *distribution research*
a ..... It is the system of sending research material to different consumers.
b ..... It is about sending out information to various research companies.
c ..... It is research into the ways products or services are distributed.
d ..... It is important when making decisions about where to locate retail outlets or where agents are needed.

5 *exploratory research*
a ..... It is about choosing the best research methods.
b ..... It is designed to help marketers understand problems.
c ..... An example of it is a detailed study of why a particular product is losing sales.
d ..... It is the study of new markets.

6 *marketing communications research*

a ..... It is the investigation of ways to talk to consumers and the public in general.

b ..... It is a kind of marketing research.

c ..... It is about the telecommunications sector.

d ..... It looks only at the results of communication methods.

7 *marketing research*

a ..... It is the same as market research.

b ..... It is about looking at the effects of advertising.

c ..... It includes market research.

d ..... It is about collecting, studying and analysing information which affects marketing decisions.

8 *omnibus survey*

a ..... It is research carried out on behalf of several companies together.

b ..... It is research on the performance of many different products.

c ..... Omnibus surveys look at several companies and compare their performance.

d ..... It is a survey which companies can buy from the government.

9 *pricing research*

a ..... It examines the relationship between price and demand.

b ..... It is about the cost of research.

c ..... It is very important, since price is a key element in determining market share.

d ..... It is about profit and loss accounts.

10 *primary research*

a ..... It is the first research that companies do.

b ..... It is the most important research into a product and its market.

c ..... It is original research carried out by a company.

d ..... It is contrasted with secondary research, which uses published information that is easily available.

11 *product research*

a ..... It looks at the market acceptance of a product.

b ..... It involves the design and concept of a product, then testing of the product, then market acceptance of the product.

c ..... It is about competitors' products.

d ..... It is principally the same as quality testing.

43 Research terms

Match each word on the left with an appropriate word on the right to make a phrase common in market research.

1	closed	a)	analysis
2	random	b)	population
3	biased	c)	trial
4	computer	d)	brief
5	clinical	e)	awareness
6	consumer	f)	sampling
7	personal	g)	interview
8	total	h)	sample
9	quota	i)	question
10	research	j)	survey

44 Research methods 1

Match the definitions (1–8) with the words and phrases (a–h).

1 A sampling method based on using small groups that are representative of much larger groups.

a) opinion poll

2 Analysis of numerical information to test that results are accurate and reliable.

b) validity

3 A limited study carried out on a small number of people to test your research methods.

c) cluster sampling

4 A survey designed to find out what people think, often on politics or environmental issues.

d) extrapolation

5 A set of questions in which the answers given affect what question(s) will be asked next.

e) statistical analysis

6 Original study carried out among the population, not by finding out information from published sources.

f) pilot survey

7 An essential quality for research. Without it, the research is not reliable.

g) fieldwork

8 Using information gained from a small number of people to estimate how large numbers of (similar) people would behave in similar circumstances.

h) unstructured survey

45 Research methods 2

Fill in the crossword. All the answers are terms used in research methods.

Across

1 A sampling method based on using small groups that are representative of much larger groups. (7, 8)

4 A test set of questions used on a small sample of people. It helps to identify problems in survey design. (5, 13)

5 A method of choosing who to use as research respondents that is based on identifying people with certain characteristics, e.g. males, aged 18–25 who drive and have above average income. (5, 8)

6 A survey designed to find out what people think – often on political issues. (7, 4)

7 Original study carried out by going out among the population to watch people, ask questions, etc. Contrast this with finding out information from published sources such as books or reports.

8 A question with a limited number of possible answers, e.g. Yes or No. (6, 8)

9 A formal design for a questionnaire which is not dependent on the answers given. (10, 6)

10 A method of selecting who will be included in a sample which ensures that the sample is representative of the whole population. (6, 8)

Down

1 A study of rival companies and their products. (10, 8)

2 A study of data using information technology hardware and software. (8, 8)

3 Questioning people individually, usually face-to-face. (8, 9)

6 A type of question which allows the person answering to use his or her own words, e.g. What do you think about Fresho Soap products? (4, 8)

1. _ _ _ _ _ S _ _ _ _ _ _
2. / 3.
4. _ _ O Q _ _ _ _ _ _ _ _ _ _
E
5. _ _ _ _ _ _ _ _ _ _ _ _
6. _ _ _ _ _ _ _ _ L _
7. _ E _ _ _ _ _
A
8. L _ _ _ _ _ _ _ _ _ _ _
9. _ _ _ T _ _ _ _ _ V _ _
10. N _ _ _ _ M _ _ _ _

46 Key words 6

Find 8 common words connected with consumers and market segmentation in the word square. You can read the words vertically (3 words) or horizontally (5 words).

P	O	S	I	T	I	O	N	I	N	G
P	B	E	K	L	M	O	G	R	G	F
O	N	G	L	D	Q	U	I	R	T	G
I	G	M	R	B	C	D	L	B	A	E
N	B	E	H	A	V	I	O	U	R	R
G	E	N	D	I	F	F	Y	N	G	D
A	E	T	H	I	C	S	A	I	E	L
N	M	G	E	L	S	P	L	M	T	E
U	S	L	I	F	E	S	T	Y	L	E
L	O	Y	M	E	N	T	Y	T	U	C
A	T	T	I	T	U	D	E	N	S	E

47 Decision making

Read the extract about the decision making process. Fill in the missing words in the sentences. Choose from the following:

differentiated marketing strategy	extensive problem solving
decision maker	positioning
decision making unit	prospects

In the field of industrial marketing, usually no one person is the (1) .... It is more likely that several individuals form a (2) ....

If the product is very specialized or complex, the selling company will need a clearly (3) .... If the product offers many benefits, the potential buyers, or (4) ...., will have many needs and many questions. They are therefore involved in (5) .... Part of this will involve making comparisons, because there are often several broadly similar competitors. Consequently, products need a clear (6) .... to make them distinctive and attractive to buyers.

48 Consumers and decision makers

Write the number of each description (1–8) and the letter of the correct picture (a–h) next to the type of consumer. (See example):

achiever	5e
belonger	......
decision maker	......
dependent	......
emulator	......
influencer	......
initiator	......
integrated	......

1 This person has a traditional outlook. He or she likes to feel comfortable but does not like change.

2 This person has the original idea to do something.

3 This person is young and fit. He or she is ambitious, determined to win in life.

4 This person is content with life, neither over-ambitious nor locked in the past.

5 This person has worked hard and got what he or she wanted.

6 This person announces that something is going to happen.

7 This person tells other people about an innovation they think is a good one.

8 This person is unable to survive well alone because of age, lack of money or a physical or mental disability.

49 Buying behaviour

Fill in the missing prepositions in the sentences. Choose from the following. Words are used more than once.

at	in	into	of	on	to	with

1 People who are concerned .... society are typically interested .... marketing ethics.
2 Niche is frequently concerned .... aiming particular products .... specific socio-economic groups.
3 Brand loyalty is based .... the development .... routine purchasing of low-involvement goods.
4 The success of shops attached .... petrol stations depends .... impulse purchasing. You can see motorists who suddenly decide to buy a music cassette, confectionery or a magazine.
5 Research .... buyer behaviour shows that when consumers make routine purchases .... regularly-used consumer products, they are not personally involved .... the products.
6 Routine purchasing contrasts .... the purchase of consumer durables, such as furniture, kitchen appliances or a car. Here there is a greater degree .... personal involvement.

50 Market segmentation 1

Mark the following statements True or False. If a statement is false, correct it.

	True	False
1 *Social marketing* targets particular consumers according to socio-economic group.	☐	☐
2 *Target marketing* is concerned with advertising to particular groups of consumers.	☐	☐
3 *Differentiated marketing* aims to appeal to specifically identified groups of potential users of a product.	☐	☐
4 *Undifferentiated marketing* is all kinds of marketing techniques used at once.	☐	☐
5 *Segmentation strategy* is an attempt to divide the total market into specific types of consumers.	☐	☐
6 *Product positioning* is a way of promoting goods in stores.	☐	☐

51 Market segmentation 2

Write the words and phrases on the next page in the right place on the table. (See examples):

Types of market segmentation		
Behaviouristic segmentation	**Benefits segmentation**	**Demographic segmentation**
use/non-use of product	*product characteristics*	*age*
Geographic segmentation	**Industrial market segmentation**	**Psychographic segmentation**
state/country	*turnover*	*opinions*

climate

ethnic origin

size of company

nationality

region

political beliefs

urban/ suburban/ rural

knowledge/ awareness of a product

leisure interests

attitudes to a product

type of company

sex

product performance

52 Key planning terms 1

A Match each word (1–5) with its opposite (a–e).

1 overseas	a) free market economy
2 strength	b) demand
3 buyer	c) domestic
4 supply	d) weakness
5 command economy	e) supplier

B Now fill in the missing words in the sentences using some of the words from part A.

1 Nabisco has dominated the .... biscuit market in the USA for over 60 years.

2 The enormous .... of the McDonald's brand name has helped the company to enter new markets all over the world.

3 A .... of small retail businesses is their inability to compete with larger competitors in fixing favourable terms with ....s.

4 Most major European manufacturers have to look to .... markets to increase their sales volume.

5 When a .... needs to purchase large quantities of goods, it is often possible to achieve important cost savings.

6 Effective pricing policy depends on the .... and .... relationship.

53 Key planning terms 2

Decide if the following terms are the same (S) or different (D). Write the answer in the box. If they are different, explain why.

1 strategy / plan ☐

2 customer / client ☐

3 marketing brief / set of objectives ☐

4 free market / market economy ☐

5 market trend / market survey ☐

6 marketing mix / advertising mix ☐

7 product mix / marketing mix ☐

8 mission statement / corporate mission ☐

9 opportunities / threats ☐

10 royalty / franchise agreement ☐

54 Marketing planning 1

Fill in the missing words in the sentences. Choose from the following:

economies of scale	external audit	marketing planning
economies of scope	marketing audit	marketing research

1 Increasing production by 25% does not increase costs by much, because we are able to take advantage of ....

2 A complete .... will demonstrate all aspects of our performance in terms of meeting our marketing objectives.

3 .... is essential to prepare clear objectives and a strategy for reaching them.

4 The .... examines factors which are not under the company's control.

5 By having documentation which can be used in various markets we are able to take advantage of ....

6 We are conducting .... to try to improve all aspects of our company performance.

55 Marketing planning 2

Choose the correct term for each of the definitions. In some cases, there are two correct answers.

1 The market consisting of the country where a company is based and no other countries.
   a servant market   b domestic market   c home market

2 Factors which 1) may have a negative affect on company performance, but which 2) are outside the company's control and 3) are identified during an analysis of marketing performance and prospects.
   a weaknesses   b threats   c competitors

3 A contract which allows another company to make your product and states the terms of payment.
   a franchise   b patent   c licence agreement

4 The action of making illegal duplicates of copyright material.
   a pirating   b cloning   c copyright infringement

5 A large company with subsidiaries in many different countries.
   a transnational   b corporation   c multinational

6 Factors which 1) probably have a negative affect on company performance, 2) are within the company's control, and 3) are identified during an analysis of marketing performance and prospects.
   a weaknesses   b threats   c failures

56 Marketing audit

Fill in the missing words in the personal letter from one director of an electrical supplies company to another. Choose from the following:

domestic	external audit	marketing audit	threat
export	internal audit	SWOT analysis	

J.A.W. Electrical Supplies Limited

P.O. Box 28,
Beech Road Industrial Estate,
Basildon SS32 1PX

12 October 19—.

Dear Isabelle,

Just a short note to bring you up-to-date while
you are away.

Since there has been a decline in our
(1) .... sales we have decided to
carry out a (2) .... to identify
areas where improvement can be made. This consists
of a typical (3) .... with an
(4) .... to look at factors within
the company and an (5) ....
examining factors outside our immediate control.
We expect that the major (6) ....
to improved performance in our domestic markets is
the weakness of the national economy.

The good news is that while home sales have
fallen, our (7) .... performance
has been good.

Please call me when you return to the office to
discuss this in more detail.

Best regards,

John

John

---

57 International marketing

Read the extract from a marketing consultant's report on options for Apsa, a Spanish food distribution company, to expand into an international market. Then fill in the missing information on the map labels.

Recommendations for Latin American expansion: Options

There are three possible ways for Apsa to expand its activities in the region.

One is to set up subsidiaries. However, this can be expensive and risky without a lot of preliminary research into the target market. International research should include finding out about the economy, local habits and customs, as well as about the markets for the products you are involved with. We suggest research of this type would be appropriate for Argentina, where establishing a subsidiary may be the best option.

An alternative is to use overseas agents and distributors. This can be effective, and is definitely much cheaper. We recommend this type of relationship in Mexico and Chile. A possible problem is conflict of interest where an agent also handles a competitor's products. We suggest Apsa should try to obtain sole distribution agreements for these countries.

A third option – probably best for Peru and Bolivia – with the advantage that it is common in the food and drinks industry, is franchising. With franchising individuals pay to use the name of a well-known manufacturer. The franchisor can insist on various policies, standards and purchasing practice, as well as receiving a payment and a regular royalty from the franchisees.

Country: ....
Preferred expansion method: ....
Advantages: ....
Possible difficulties: ....
Recommendation: ....

Country: ....
Preferred expansion method: ....
Advantages: ....
Sources of income: ....

Country: ....
Preferred expansion method: ....
Advantages: ....
Sources of income: ....

Country: ....
Preferred expansion method: ....
Advantages: ....
Possible difficulties: ....
Recommendation: ....

Country: ....
Preferred expansion method: ....
Disadvantages: ....
Recommendation: ....

58 Growth-share matrix

Read the extract from a training seminar on the Growth-share matrix and study the diagram. Then mark the statements (1–6) True or False. If they are false, explain why.

CASH GENERATION
(market share)

	HIGH	LOW
HIGH	STAR ☆	QUESTION MARK ? support to convert to 'star'?
LOW	CASH COW	→ → DOG Net cash users Abandon?

CASH USE
(growth rate)

Illustration reproduced by permission © Boston Consulting Group.

The Growth-Share Matrix

The growth-share matrix was originally conceived by the Boston Consulting Group. It is basically a tool to help marketeers decide which products need extra support – in terms of cash investment – and which should be dropped completely.

Cash Cows are the dream product: they generate high income but don't actually require a lot of spending. A Cash Cow product practically markets itself. A Star, on the other hand, is a new product, it requires a lot of cash, the advertising budget is high. You hope it might become a Cash Cow, but for now it offers a possibly very high short-term profit.

Question Marks, also known as problem products, probably need a lot of cash investment to turn them into Stars. On the other hand, they may never be really successful.

At least the choice is usually clearer with Dogs: they don't use much cash, but they don't generate much income, either; they can probably be dropped.

	True	False
1 Cash Cows make a lot of money.	☐	☐
2 Products shown to be Dogs in the growth-share matrix usually need a lot of money spending on them. Perhaps they are not worth it.	☐	☐
3 Stars can make good short-term profits even though they use a lot of cash.	☐	☐
4 The growth-share matrix is a planning tool designed to show which products need extra marketing support and which should be abandoned.	☐	☐
5 Question Marks are also known as problem products.	☐	☐
6 Companies need to make a decision on what to do with Question Marks – they might develop into Stars if given extra support.	☐	☐

Answers

Test 1

R	Q	A	I	J	K	L	M	P	L	A	N
C	U	S	T	O	M	E	R	N	P	O	Q
S	A	A	M	A	R	K	E	T	N	G
H	L	B	L	F	G	H	J	S	T	O
O	I	F	E	F	W	R	U	C	V	O
J	T	G	A	G	Y	B	B	C	E	A	D
L	Y	H	T	H	R	U	B	D	U	S
N	Q	R	P	R	O	D	U	C	T	Q	P
O	S	I	T	R	V	G	H	J	W	R
O	M	S	E	R	V	I	C	E	S	X	E
D	K	I	R	E	S	E	A	R	C	H
D	X	X	A	P	Q	U	A	N	A	F	H

Test 2

1 product
2 place
3 time
4 needs
5 profit
6 customers
7 want
8 producing
9 developing
10 product
11 service
12 price
13 promote
14 distribute

Test 3

1	market	marketer	market, marketing
2	distribute	distributor	distribution
3	compete	competitor	competition
4	advertise	advertiser	advertising, advertisement
5	supply	supplier	supply
6	sponsor	sponsor	sponsorship
7	consume	consumer	consumption
8	produce	producer	product
9	analyse	analyst	analysis
10	research	researcher	research
11	import	importer	import

Test 4

1 goods
2 free
3 research
4 demand
5 mix
6 plan
7 trends
8 analysis

Test 5

1 (c) sponsorship
2 (a) marketing consultancy
3 (c) free market economy
4 (b) buyer's market
5 (b) seller's market
6 (c) market leader
7 (a) market analyst
8 (a) campaign
9 (b) distribution, or possibly (a) shipment
10 (b) exporting
11 (c) market share

Test 6

1 plan
2 strengths
3 weaknesses
4 opportunities
5 threats
6 mix
7 product
8 place
9 price / promotion / packaging
10 promotion / packaging / price
11 packaging / price / promotion

Test 7

1 Product
2 Price
3 Place
4 Promotion
5 People
6 Packaging
7 Phasing

Test 8

f Well, we identified five areas where improvement is necessary.

h The first is product.

b It covers both goods and services offered by the company.

e The second area is place – also called distribution – meaning the movement of goods from the producer to the customer.

g After place, packaging. Packaging includes the packaging materials but, more importantly, all

types of added value and customer expectations.
a And then the fourth area is phasing.
d Yes, or timing – getting things where they
should be at the right time.
i Promotion.
c Exactly – and the desire to buy the product.
And, finally, people, which means colleagues,
employees, agents and customers. The idea is
to keep everyone happy, make personal
contact.

SECTION 2: PRODUCT

Test 9
augmented product 5g
clone 3f
consumer durable 4b
core product 6i
fast moving consumer goods 2h
generic product 7a
perishables 1d
primary manufacturing 10c
sell-by date 9j
service 8e

Test 10
A
1 brand identity
2 brand name
3 brand image
4 own-brand
5 brand valuation
6 unbranded
7 intangible assets
8 loyalty
9 premium brand
B
1 name
2 valuation
3 unbranded
4 image
5 own-brand
6 intangible
7 loyalty
8 premium
9 identity

Test 11
1 c
2 a
3 b
4 b
5 c
6 a
7 b

Test 12
1 ... and extended five-year warranty with
absolute confidence.
2 ... but the augmented package includes four
types of software, five product manuals, a self-
help guide, free on-site warranty and the
prestige of the Triple X brand name.
3 ... before being joined by me-too products from
our competitors.
4 ... and the product was finally launched this
year.
5 Our R & D department designed the Triple X
PC48655 over a five-year period ...
6 The core product is, of course, a personal
computer ...
7 Furthermore, we expect the product to experience rapid early sales for at least three years ...
8 Of course, all components used in the
manufacture of the Triple X PC48655 have
been well tested.
9 We offer a full after sales service ...

Test 13
1 launched
2 parts/labour
3 labour/parts
4 warranty
5 state-of-the-art
6 after-sales
7 network
8 customer
9 helpline

Test 14
1 consumer
2 perishable
3 products
4 durables
5 added
6 retailer
7 service
8 purchased
9 patent
10 flop

Test 15
1 positioning
2 launch
3 product life cycle
4 product failure
5 product classification
6 product mix

Test 16
1 off
2 by

3 away
4 back
5 onto
6 on
7 to
8 into

SECTION 3: PRICE

Test 17

A	P	R	I	C	E	L	T
D	I	S	C	O	U	N	T
E	C	R	G	S	N	O	I
M	P	O	R	T	E	V	F
A	W	R	M	S	V	I	O
N	I	P	F	E	E	O	R
D	R	L	M	H	R	G	P
A	M	A	R	G	I	N	E

Test 18

A
1 e
2 c
3 d
4 b
5 a

B
1 a
2 d
3 b
4 e
5 c

Test 19
1 False. *Budget priced goods* are low-priced goods.
2 True
3 True
4 True
5 True
6 False. The *factory gate price* is the price a manufacturer asks when selling a product to a wholesaler, agent or retailer.
7 False. *Production* costs are all the expenses a manufacturer has to pay to produce a product, including labour.
8 False. The *market price* is the typical price that different companies are asking for similar products.
9 True
10 True
11 False. The *wholesale price* is the price a retailer pays a wholesaler for a product.

Test 20
1 unit cost
2 retail margin
3 selling costs
4 price war
5 budget priced
6 going rate
7 demand curve

Test 21
1 c
2 f
3 a
4 e
5 g
6 b
7 d

Test 22
1 a
2 c
3 a
4 b
5 b
6 a
7 b
8 c
9 a
10 a
11 b
12 a

Test 23
1 advanced orders
2 break even
3 Production costs
4 high penetration
5 premium price
6 recommended retail
7 factory gate
8 price war

SECTION 4: PLACE

Test 24
1 agent
2 distributor
3 sales representative
4 retailer
5 intermediary
6 wholesaler
7 dealer
8 exporter
9 customer
10 consumer
11 user

Test 25

1 hypermarket
2 telesales operator
3 haulage contractor
4 retailer
5 production plant
6 door-to-door salesperson
7 wholesaler
8 air freight operator
9 shipping line

Test 26

1 producer
2 consumers
3 wholesalers
4 middlemen
5 sales forces
6 sales representatives
7 despatch
8 retailers
9 multiples

Test 27

1 producer
2 haulage company
3 distributor
4 agent
5 sales representative
6 retailer
7 customer

Test 28

1 despatch rider
2 road haulage
3 barge
4 rail freight
5 container ship
6 air freight

Test 29

1 mail order companies
2 warehouses
3 large multiples
4 purchasing power
5 franchises
6 door-to-door selling
7 commission
8 mail order
9 telesales staff
10 cold calling
11 hypermarkets
12 specialist retailers
13 chain stores

Test 30

1 commission agent

2 distribution agreement
3 sales force
4 container port
5 independent distributor
6 electronic trading
7 shelf space
8 franchise agreement
9 vending machine
10 shipping line

Test 31

1 conventional marketing system (CMS)
2 vertical marketing system (VMS)
3 total systems approach (TSA)

SECTION 5: PROMOTION

Test 32

1 slogan
2 discount
3 reply coupon
4 competition
5 mass media
6 commercial
7 point-of-sale advertising
8 target audience
9 mailing list

Test 33

1 catalogue
2 hard sell
3 competition
4 impulse buying
5 campaign
6 consumer awareness
7 advertising mix
8 commercials
9 advertisements
10 direct mail
11 mail shot

Test 34

1 c
2 b
3 f
4 d
5 a
6 g
7 e

Test 35

1 unique selling proposition
2 publicity
3 rational appeal
4 emotional appeal
5 targets, promotes

6 consumers

Test 36
1 direct mailing
2 direct selling
3 in-store promotion
4 on-pack promotion
5 perimeter advertising
6 BOGOF

Test 37
1 TV commercial
2 sandwich board
3 freebie
4 offer
5 banner towing
6 T-shirt advertising
7 sponsorship
8 billboard

Test 38
1 d
2 f
3 a
4 e
5 c
6 b

SECTION 6: MARKET RESEARCH

Test 39
1 survey
2 market researcher
3 poll
4 sample
5 questionnaire
6 data
7 bias
8 subject
9 respondent

Test 40
1 True
2 True
3 False. The age range covered was 15-20.
4 True
5 False. 15% claim to eat reasonably healthy foods most of the time; 6% claimed they always ate reasonably healthy foods.
6 False. This is not clear from the results.
7 True
8 True

Test 41
1 market research
2 market research brief

3 causal research study
4 consumer research
5 consumer panels
6 representative
7 population
8 questionnaire
9 pilot questionnaire
10 observational research
11 consumer awareness
12 advertising research
13 in-house research
14 secondary research

Test 42
1 agency research
 a) F, b) T, c) T, d) F
2 clinical trial
 a) F, b) T, c) T, d) F
3 desk research
 a) T, b) T, c) F, d) F
4 distribution research
 a) F, b) F, c) T, d) T
5 exploratory research
 a) F, b) T, c) T, d) F
6 marketing communications research
 a) T, b) T, c) F, d) F
7 marketing research
 a) F, b) F, c) T, d) T
8 omnibus survey
 a) T, b) T, c) F, d) F
9 pricing research
 a) T, b) F, c) T, d) F
10 primary research
 a) F, b) F, c) T, d) T
11 product research
 a) T, b) T, c) F, d) F

Test 43
1 i
2 h
3 j
4 a
5 c
6 e
7 g
8 b
9 f
10 d

Test 44
1 c
2 e
3 f
4 a
5 h
6 g

7 b
8 d

Test 45

Across
1 cluster sampling
4 pilot questionnaire
5 quota sampling
6 opinion poll
7 fieldwork
8 closed question
9 structured survey
10 random sampling

Down
1 competitor analysis
2 computer analysis
3 personal interview
6 open question

SECTION 7: CONSUMERS AND MARKET SEGMENTATION

Test 46

P	O	S	I	T	I	O	N	I	N	G
P	B	E	K	L	M	O	G	R	G	F
O	N	G	L	D	Q	U	I	R	T	G
I	G	M	R	B	C	D	L	B	A	E
N	B	E	H	A	V	I	O	U	R	R
G	E	N	D	I	F	F	Y	N	G	D
A	E	T	H	I	C	S	A	I	E	L
N	M	G	E	L	S	P	L	M	T	E
U	S	L	I	F	E	S	T	Y	L	E
L	O	Y	M	E	N	T	Y	T	U	C
A	T	T	I	T	U	D	E	N	S	E

Test 47
1 decision maker
2 decision making unit
3 differentiated marketing strategy
4 prospects
5 extensive problem solving
6 positioning

Test 48
achiever 5e
belonger 1d
decision maker 6h
dependent 8b
emulator 3a
influencer 7f
initiator 2g
integrated 4c

Test 49
1 with, in
2 with, at

3 on, of
4 to, on
5 into, of, in
6 with, of

Test 50
1 False. Social marketing takes general attitudes in society into account in all marketing decisions, e.g. cruelty to animals is wrong, the environment has to be protected, men look after the children.
2 False. Target marketing is concerned with making sure a product is appropriate for specifically identified needs.
3 True
4 False. Undifferentiated marketing is aimed at everyone in society. It promotes a product and its reputation for everyone, not just users.
5 True
6 False. Product positioning aims to ensure that a product has unique and distinguishing features, appealing to particular consumers.

Test 51

Types of market segmentation		
Behaviouristic segmentation	**Benefits segmentation**	**Demographic segmentation**
use/non-use of product	product characteristics	age
knowledge / awareness of product	product performance	sex
attitudes to a product		ethnic origin
		nationality
Geographic segmentation	**Industrial market segmentation**	**Psychographic segmentation**
state/country	turnover	opinions
urban / surburban	type of company	political beliefs
rural	size of company	leisure interests\
region		
climate		

SECTION 8: PLANNING AND INTERNATIONAL MARKETING

Test 52
A
1 c

2 d
3 e
4 b
5 a

B

1 domestic
2 strength
3 weakness, supplier
4 overseas
5 buyer
6 supply, demand

Test 53

1 Same
2 Different. A client buys a service; a customer buys a product.
3 Same
4 Same
5 Different. A survey investigates a market; a trend is the direction something is moving in, e.g. sales.
6 Different. Marketing mix is all aspects of marketing; the advertising mix is the combination of advertising techniques.
7 Different. Product mix is the variety of products on offer from a certain company; the marketing mix is the combination of factors involved in how a company markets itself.
8 Same
9 Different. Opportunities are positive; threats are negative.
10 Different. A royalty is a commission paid on the number of sales; a franchise agreement is an agreement to use a famous product identity, logo, name, marketing approach, etc.

Test 54

1 economies of scale
2 marketing audit
3 marketing planning
4 external audit
5 economies of scope
6 marketing research

Test 55

1 b) domestic market or c) home market
2 b) threats or possibly c) competitors (these are one type of threat)
3 a) franchise or c) licence agreement
4 a) pirating or c) copyright infringement
5 c) multinational or b) corporation
6 a) weaknesses

Test 56

1 domestic
2 marketing audit
3 SWOT analysis
4 internal audit
5 external audit
6 threat
7 export

Test 57

1 Country: Mexico
   Preferred expansion method: agents and distributors
   Advantages: effective, cheaper
   Possible difficulties: conflict of agent's interests
   Recommendation: obtain sole distribution agreement.
2 Country: Peru
   Preferred expansion method: franchising
   Advantages: common in food and drink industry
   Sources of income: payment, regular royalties
3 Country: Bolivia
   Preferred expansion method: franchising
   Advantages: common in food and drink industry
   Sources of income: payment, regular royalties
4 Country: Chile
   Preferred expansion method: agents and distributors
   Advantages: effective, cheaper
   Possible difficulties: conflict of agent's interests
   Recommendation: obtain sole distribution agreement.
5 Country: Argentina
   Preferred expansion method: subsidiary
   Disadvantages: expensive, risky
   Recommendation: do a lot of preliminary research

Test 58

1 True
2 False. Usually the opposite: to drop them, spend no money.
3 True. *Stars* can make good short term profits and may become *Cash Cows*, therefore producing long term profits.
4 True
5 True
6 True

Word List

The numbers after the entries are the tests in which they appear.

A

above-the-line promotion, 34
achiever, 48
added value, 8, 14
advanced orders, 23
advertise, 3
advertisement, 3, 33
advertiser, 3
advertising (n), 3, 32
advertising mix, 33, 53
advertising research, 41
after-sales network, 13
after-sales service, 12
agency research, 42
agent, 24, 27, 57
AIDA, 34
air freight, 28
air freight operator, 25
analyse, 3
analysis, 3, 4, 43
analyst, 3
attitude, 46
augmented package, 12
augmented product, 9, 11

B

banner towing, 37
bargain selling, 36
barge, 28
behaviour, 46, 49
behaviouristic segmentation, 51
belonger, 48
below-the-line promotion, 34
benefits segmentation, 51
bias, 39, 40, 43
billboard, 37
BOGOF, 36
brand identity, 8, 10
brand image, 10
brand name, 10, 12
brand valuation, 10
break even, 23
break-even point, 21
brief (n), 43
budget priced, 18, 19, 20
buyer, 52
buyer's market, 5

C

campaign, 5, 33
cannibalism, 11
Cash Cow, 58
cash generation, 58
catalogue, 33
causal research, 41
chain, 26
chain store, 29
client, 53
clinical trial, 42
clone, 9
cloning, 55
closed question, 45
cluster sampling, 44, 45
cold calling, 29
command economy, 52
commercial (n), 32, 33, 37
commission, 22, 29
commission agent, 30
compete, 3
competition, 3, 32, 33
competitor, 3, 55
competitor analysis, 45
component, 12
computer analysis, 45
conflict of interest, 57
consume, 3,
consumer, 3, 14, 24, 26, 35, 43
consumer awareness, 8, 33, 41
consumer durable, 9, 14, 49
consumer panel, 41
consumer research, 41
consumption, 3
container port, 30
container ship, 28
conventional marketing system, 31
copyright infringement, 55
core product, 9, 12
corporate image, 38
corporate mission, 53
corporation, 55
cost of labour, 22
cost of production, 22
cost of sales, 22
costs, 17
customer, 1, 2, 24, 26, 27, 53
customer expectations, 8

produce (v), 2, 3
producer, 3, 26, 27
product, 1, 2, 3, 6, 7, 8, 14
product classification, 15
product failure, 15
production costs, 19, 23
production plant, 25
product lifecycle, 11, 15
product mix, 15, 53
product positioning, 50
product research, 42
profit, 2, 17
promote, 2, 35
promotion, 6, 7, 8
prospect, 47
psychographic segmentation, 51
publicity, 35
purchase (n), 49
purchase (v), 14
purchasing power, 29
push strategy, 34

Q

quality, 1
Question Mark, 58
questionnaire, 39, 41
quota sampling, 45

R

R & D, 12
rail freight, 28
random sample, 40
random sampling, 45
rational appeal, 35
recommended retail price, 19, 23
reply coupon, 32
representative (adj), 41
research (n), 1, 3, 4, 41, 42, 43, 49
research (v), 3
researcher, 3
respondent, 39, 40
retailer, 14, 24, 25, 26, 27
retail price, 19, 23
revenue, 17
road haulage, 28
royalty, 53, 57

S

sales force, 26, 30
sales representative, 24, 26, 27
sales team, 26
sample, 39, 43
sampling, 43

sandwich board, 37
secondary research, 41
segment, 46
segmentation strategy, 50
sell-by date, 9, 11,
seller's market, 5
selling costs, 20, 22
service (n), 2, 9
service industry, 14
services, 1, 8
set of objectives, 53
shelf space, 30
shipment, 5, 26
shipping line, 25, 30
short-term profit, 58
skimming strategy, 18
slogan, 32
social group, 40
social marketing, 50
social status, 40
socio-economic group, 40, 49
sole distribution agreement, 57
specialist retailer, 29
special offer, 36
sponsor (n), 3
sponsor (v), 3
sponsorship, 3, 5, 36, 37
Star, 58
state-of-the-art, 13
statistical analysis, 44
status group, 40
strategy, 53
strength, 6, 52
structured survey, 45
subject, 39
subsidiary, 57
supplier, 3, 52
supply (n), 3, 52
supply (v), 3
survey, 39, 40, 44
SWOT analysis, 6, 56

T

target (v), 35, 40, 46
target audience, 32
target marketing, 50
telephone interview, 40
telesales operator, 25
telesales staff, 29
threat, 56
threats, 6, 53, 55
time, 2
timing, 8
total systems approach, 31
trend, 4, 40